Recorder Duets
from the Beginning

3

John Pitts

Duet playing brings extra pleasure to all involved, and with it an incentive to learn new notes and rhythms in order to succeed. A simultaneous development of listening skills and concentration is also required for successful ensemble playing.

Recorder Duets from the Beginning Books 1, 2 and *3* provide a wide range of repertoire to encourage duet playing by descant recorder players, both accompanied and unaccompanied. All the items are carefully graded, both in range of notes (pitches) included and in the level of difficulty. It is expected that players using Book 3 will have already reached the end of *Recorder from the Beginning Book 2* and started *Book 3*, in the author's widely popular teaching scheme.

The Pupil's Books include guitar chord symbols, and the Latin American items have suggestions for use of percussion instruments. The Teacher's Books include piano accompaniments for all the duets as well as the Latin American percussion parts.

In keeping with the 'repertoire' nature of the books, only a minimum of teaching help or explanation is given. Where more help is required it is best to refer to the appropriate pages of the teaching scheme *Recorder from the Beginning*.

Contents

*Notes listed as 'included' do not necessarily appear often in the piece.
Some may occur only once or twice in a piece!
It is best to assess each item individually.

The 'repertoire' items usually use a restricted note range, and can be played
at any stage when players have the incentive to learn and enjoy a new piece.

To a Wild Rose   Edward MacDowell

2 = optional alternative fingering, see page 32.

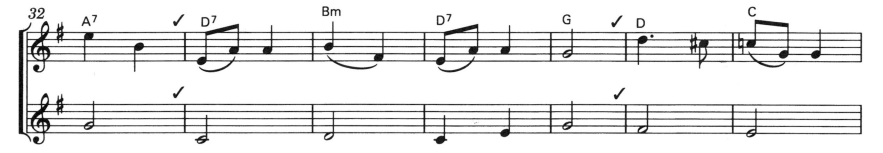

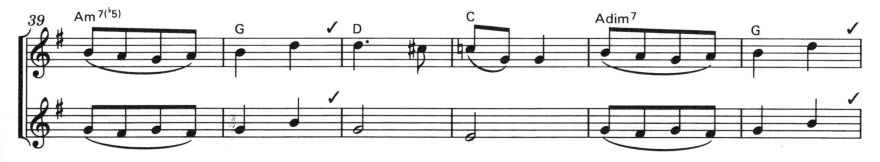

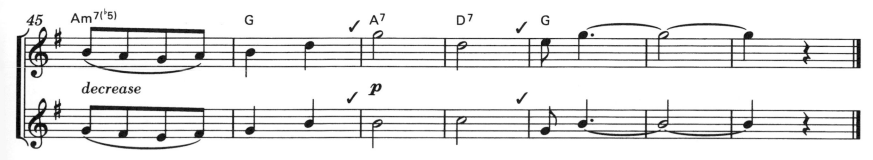

Andante Grazioso   Mozart

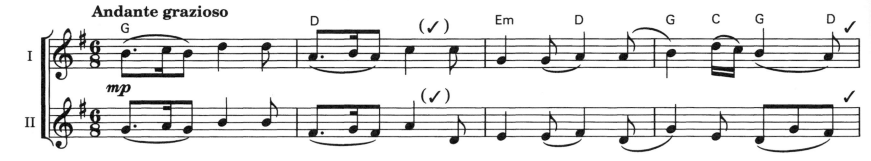

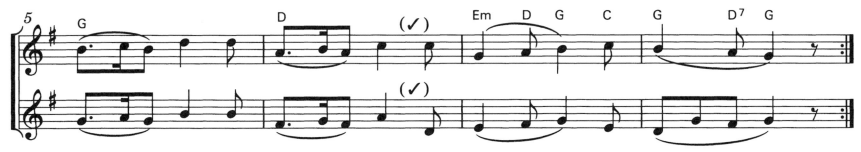

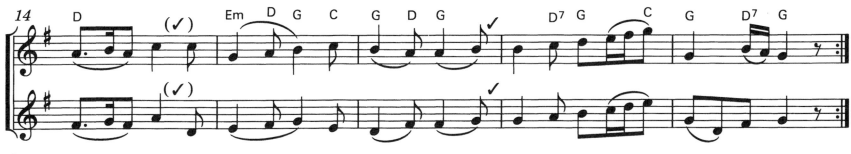

Soldier's March   Schumann

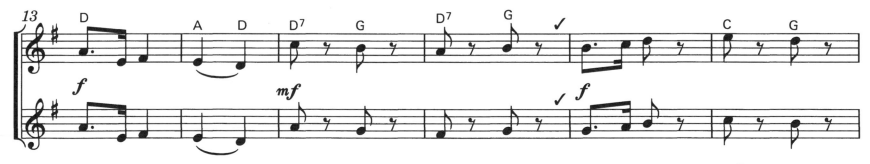

Beckett Blues   Pitts

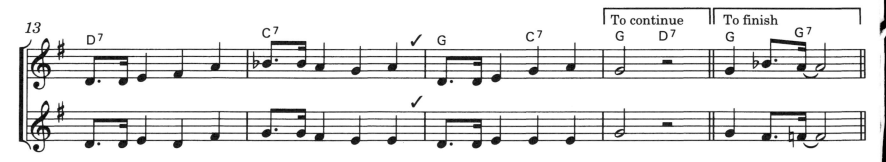

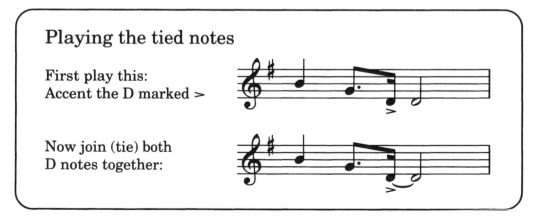

Playing the tied notes

First play this:
Accent the D marked >

Now join (tie) both
D notes together:

*For D♯ see page 32.

Polovtsian Dances   Borodin

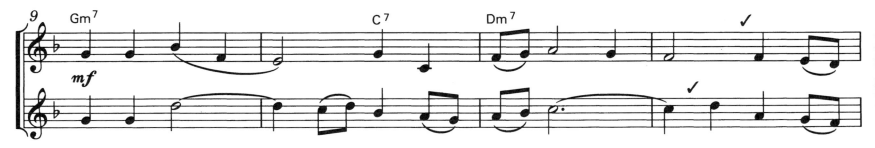

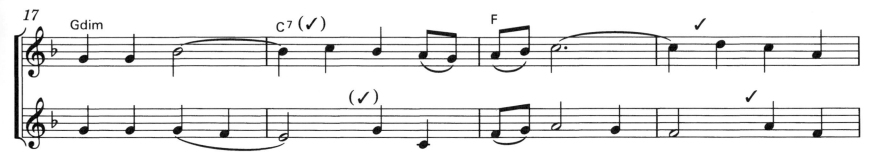

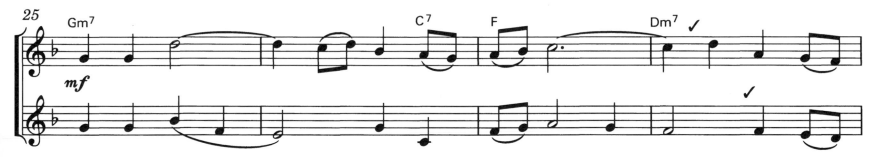

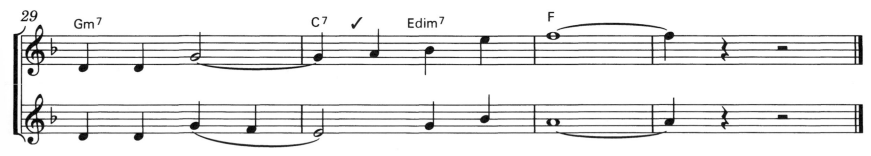

Summertime *   George Gershwin

George **Gershwin** (1898 - 1937) was an American composer who successfully combined popular, jazz and serious orchestral music into a new style. 'Summertime' is from the popular folk opera 'Porgy and Bess'*. Other works include 'Rhapsody in Blue' and 'An American in Paris'.

*Written in collaboration with DuBose and Dorothy Heyward and Ira Gershwin.

Largo   Corelli

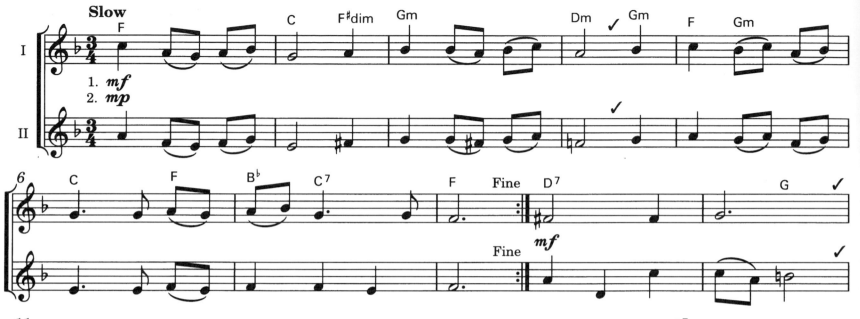

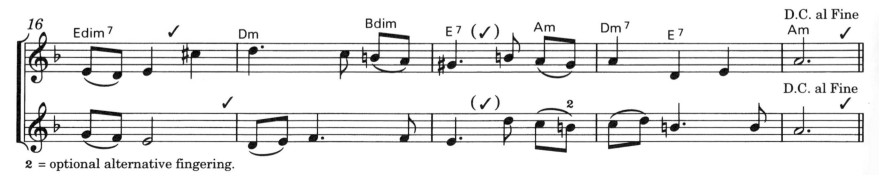

2 = optional alternative fingering.

The Lorelei   German

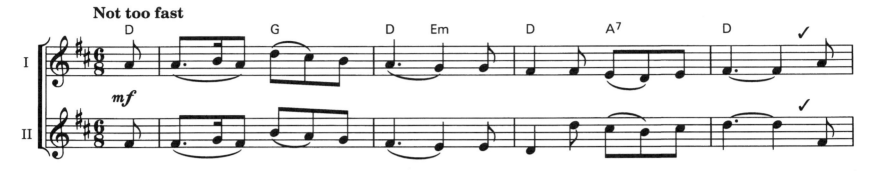

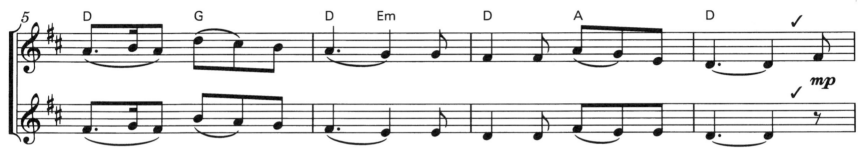

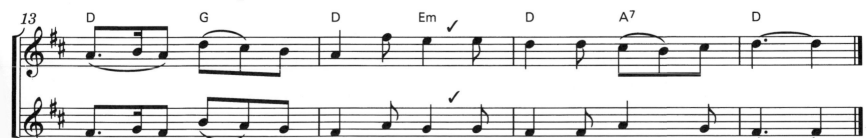

American Patrol   F.W. Meacham

2 = optional alternative fingering.

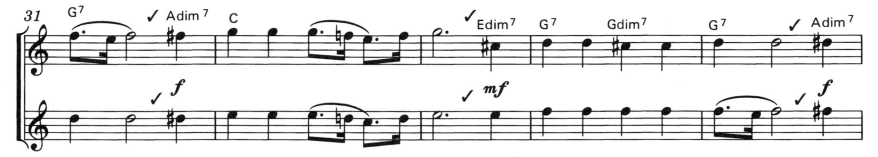

Las Heras Beguine   Pitts

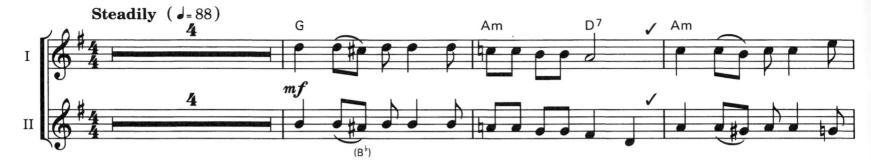

The **beguine** is a Latin American fox-trot dance. The melody is usually fairly smooth and regular, with the characteristic beguine rhythms played in the accompaniment. A simple fox-trot bass is combined with an off-beat eighth-note (quaver) rhythm. An accented second eighth-note in each bar helps to give the dance its particular character.

Two people can combine to play this beguine accompaniment.

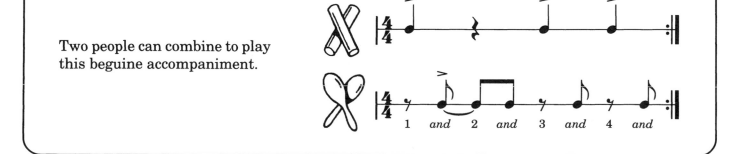

Andante   Mendelssohn

Medium pace

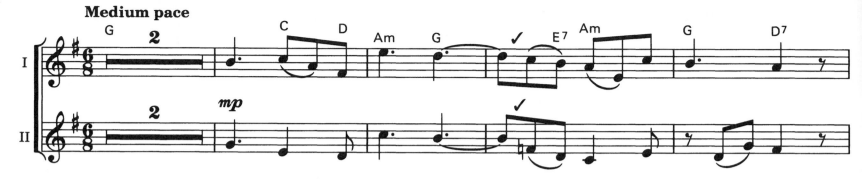

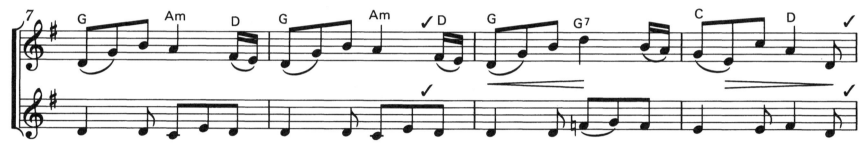

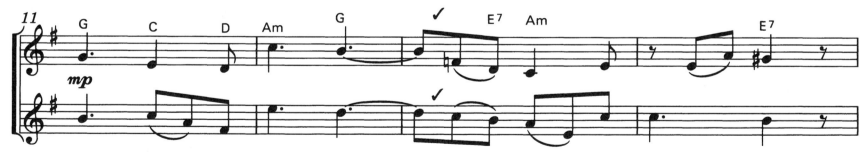

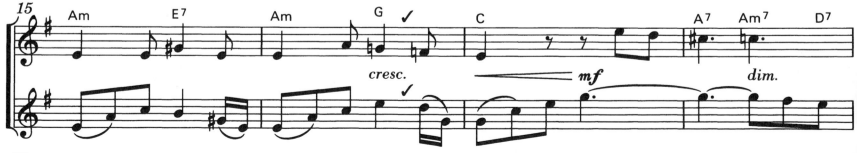

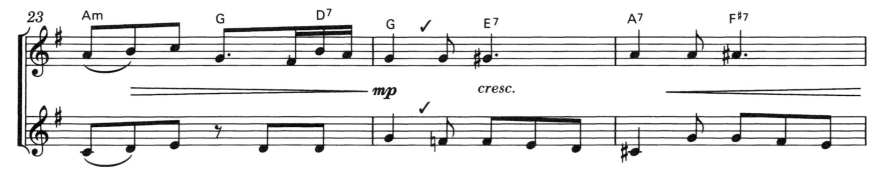

Felix **Mendelssohn** (1809 - 1847) was a German composer. His orchestral music includes the popular 'Hebrides' overture, and his choral music includes the oratorio 'Elijah'. The Andante used here is taken from his famous Violin Concerto in E minor.

Fear No Danger   Purcell

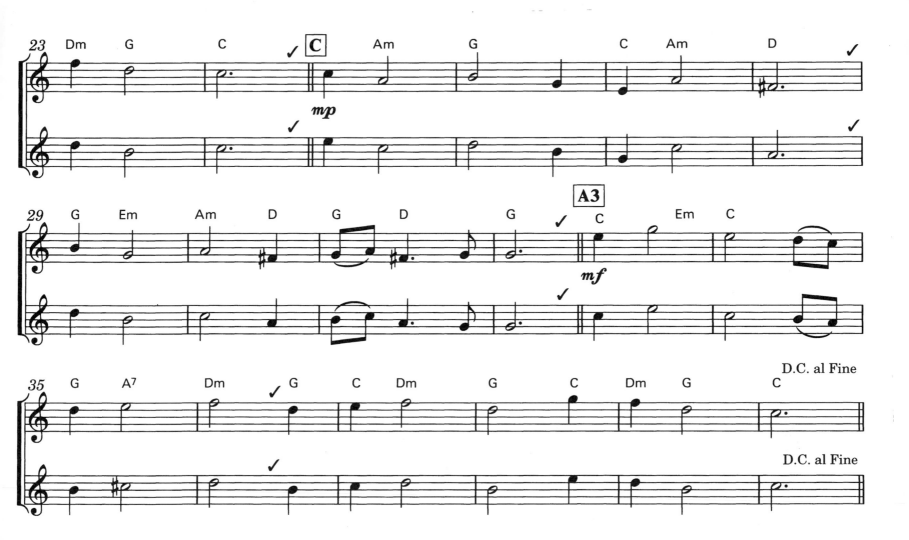

This piece is a vocal duet from Purcell's opera 'Dido and Aeneas', written in London in 1689. This particular duet uses a musical form called a **rondo.** The first tune **A** returns twice later on at **A2** and **A3** . Two contrasting passages called 'episodes' (tunes **B** and **C**) separate the returns of the main tune **A** . So a rondo can be described as an **A B A C A** form.

The piece by Mozart on page 30 has RONDO as its title.

Yellow Bird Calypso

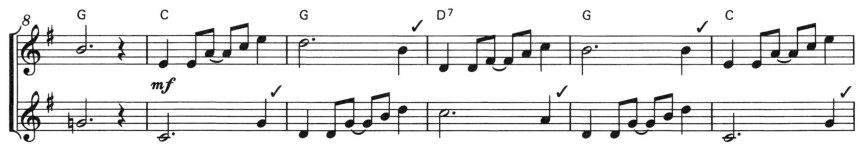

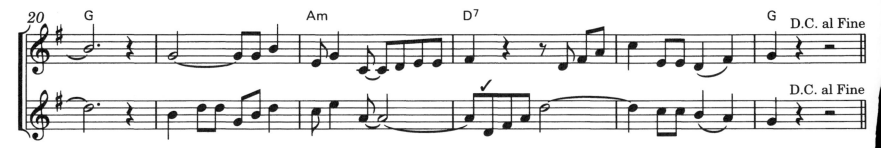

Peacherine Rag   Scott Joplin

La Paloma Yradier

Habaneras by the Spanish composer Sebastien **Yradier** (1809 -1865) inspired Bizet to write the Habanera in 'Carmen' (see page 28).

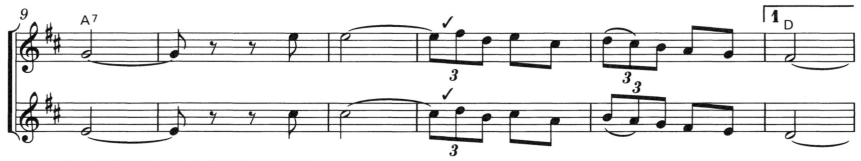

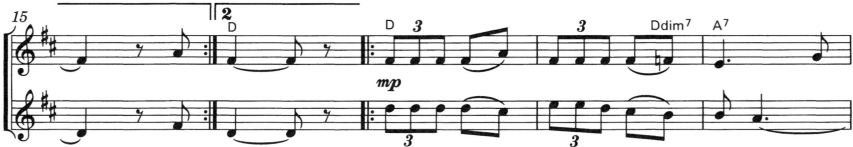

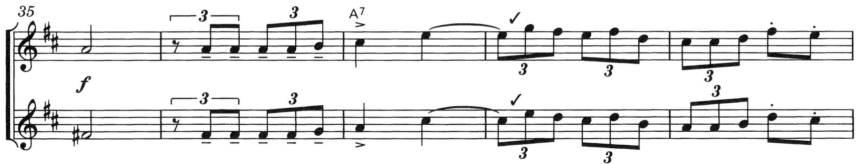

Habanera from Carmen   Bizet

Rondo Mozart

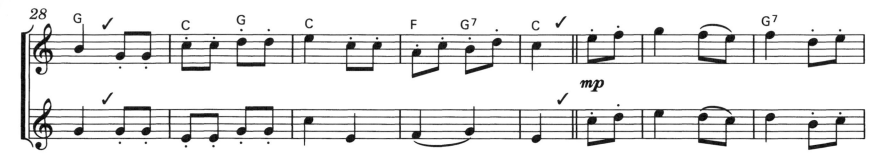

D.C. no repeats to Coda

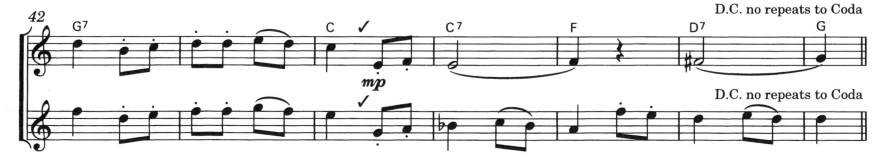

D.C. no repeats to Coda

Fingering Chart
English (Baroque) Fingered Recorders

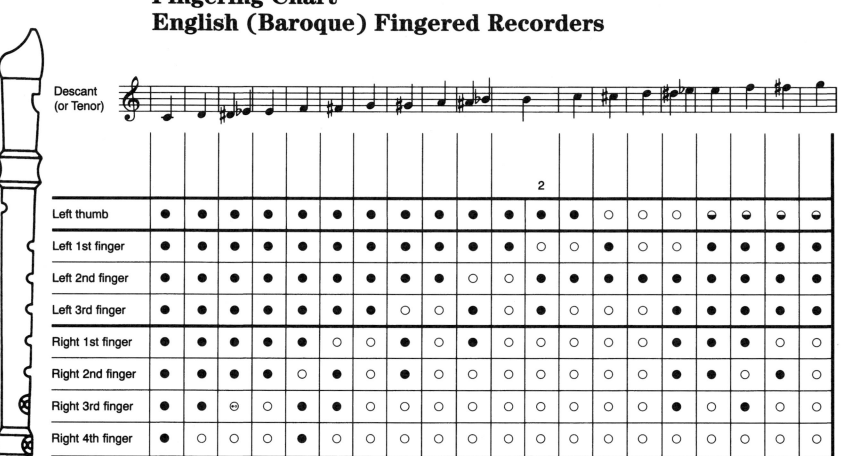

Descant (or Tenor)

Left thumb	●	●	●	●	●	●	●	●	●	●	●	●	●	○	○	○	◒	◒	◒	◒
Left 1st finger	●	●	●	●	●	●	●	●	●	●	●	○	○	●	○	○	●	●	●	●
Left 2nd finger	●	●	●	●	●	●	●	●	●	○	○	●	●	●	●	●	●	●	●	●
Left 3rd finger	●	●	●	●	●	●	●	○	○	●	○	●	○	○	○	●	●	●	●	●
Right 1st finger	●	●	●	●	●	○	○	●	○	●	○	○	○	○	○	●	●	●	○	○
Right 2nd finger	●	●	●	●	○	○	○	○	○	○	○	○	○	○	●	●	○	●	○	
Right 3rd finger	●	●	◎	○	●	●	○	○	○	○	○	○	○	○	○	●	○	●	○	○
Right 4th finger	●	○	○	○	●	○	○	○	○	○	○	○	○	○	○	○	○	○	○	○

○ Open hole

● Closed hole

◒ Partly closed hole

2 Alternative fingering